SILENT ROOM

MICHAEL HELMUTH

Silent Room
Copyright © 2025 by Michael Helmuth.

This publication contains the opinions and ideas of its author. It is intended to provide helpful and informative material on the subjects addressed in the publication. The author and publisher specifically disclaim all responsibility for any liability, loss, or risk, personal or otherwise, which is incurred as a consequence, directly or indirectly, of the use and application of any of the contents of this book.

WRITERS REPUBLIC L.L.C.
515 Summit Ave. Unit R1
Union City, NJ 07087, USA

Website: *www.writersrepublic.com*
Hotline: *1-877-656-6838*
Email: *info@writersrepublic.com*

Ordering Information:
Quantity sales. Special discounts are available on quantity purchases by corporations, associations, and others. For details, contact the publisher at the address above.

Library of Congress Control Number:		2024913566	
ISBN-13:	979-8-89285-172-5	[Paperback Edition]
	979-8-89285-173-2	[Hardback Edition]
	979-8-89285-171-8	[Digital Edition]

Rev. date: 01/07/2025

PROLOGUE

I realize that no one's circumstances are completely unique except in the details. I am no exception. I have felt, for a long time, that there is something out there that I am searching for. I believe this to be true, but I don't know it for certain.

As a young boy I was incredibly shy and usually did not talk much. I learned through observation primarily up until I was about to hit puberty. Even then, social learning felt secondary to me.

What is the point of this context? I want to highlight the fact that not everyone understands things in the same way. Although my words make sense to me they may not always make sense to you and vice versa.

Not all things need to be understood to be meaningful, though. I will expound later. Just keep in mind that whatever reason it is that you decided to read this is just as valid for having no reason at all.

I had very little understanding of how things worked up until I was around 12. That is when I began to question why I knew so little about everything. It wasn't until much later that I realized that it was because everything that I knew was simply observational; I had no relative perspective to compare my knowledge to up until that age.

Before that, we moved around a lot. I would eventually get used to making temporary friends. When I finally was settled into a town I could call home, I discovered lasting friendships which I cherished more than anything. After all, I had never experienced having friends for any longer than a year or two.

Sometimes we overlook some of the simplest aspects in our lives simply because we don't know of life any differently. Hopefully you will take my words to heart when I say that even the smallest of things can be just as important as the biggest moments. Just don't take that as an excuse to make a big deal out of things because hiccups happen in life, they are always there.

SILENT ROOM

As a dialogue to introduce what the future pages hold, I would like to tell you of the purpose of this text. Sitting alone in the silence of my small apartment, I find myself face to face with a deadly adversary. Loneliness. I realize that by taking a step back and seeing this from a broader perspective I maintain a certain level of sanity and even tranquility, but there are many people who trap themselves in their own minds and break down because of it. The following passages are trains of thought which have guided me at one point or another to climb out of a dark pit of despair, conquer my innermost demons, and find peace in many aspects of life.

The purpose of this is not to persuade you to believe the world works the way that I think it does. It would be best to look at my words as an expression of my own search for meaning in the circumstances I find myself in.

The word choice I use is not meant to be political, and should be treated as conversational. Do not mistake inaccuracy or preferred words for intentional triggering; I write as a means to clear my thoughts which are not entirely of concern to the reality in which we live.

I do discuss reality at length sometimes, but just keep in mind that I am not presenting an argument, just revealing a train of thought. Come aboard if you're curious.

I number each train of thought, not chronologically nor to represent the level of quality, but to separate each train of thought and to make it easier for the reader to distinguish between these. Most of these are self contained, which means that if you find contradiction between separate trains of thought, it is because those two ideas have not been considered by each other. Yet.

I know I'm not the most or best at anything in particular, but I know at least a few things.

I know that I am real. I experience reality to some capacity, and how could I experience anything if I wasn't real to some extent? Regardless of the notion that a simulative existence may possibly be our reality, it fails to describe to me a way in which we do not exist. A simulation is a simulation, not nothingness. You exist. But that doesn't give you the answers as to why that is the case.

Another thing that I know is that the structures of the societies of our world-governments, institutions, religions, economies, cultures, and so forth – are structures created by mankind. That isn't to say that my point invalidates their existence, just that if we are to obtain new ideas we must think outside of these structures. There are rules in place that make life better in general such as the command against murder, theft, and cheating. To universalize such crimes would be impossible to accomplish without destroying the bonds of all of our neighbors, family, and friends. However, I still suggest thinking outside of the structures which add on to complications of life; the natural structure of our lives should be of common sense but there are factors which complicate things regardless of such simplicity.

I might decide to live a life according to some higher order whose likeness is that of a father in either literal or religious senses and force myself to abide by rules of my own choosing because I do not know what rules such a higher order may command of me. I cannot ask my father what rules he follows for life if he passes away, nor can I ask him if something clouds his judgment and prevents him from giving me sound advice. I cannot ask God for rules to live life. Though there are the ten commandments it does not account for the complications of human existence. What then, am I to do? Perhaps the answer is to reverse thinking in this regard. I may act in a way that may make me proud if I was my own son. Would I be proud of my son if he acted as I do right now?

I often find tranquility and zeal in my life thinking this way. The world may be better because of it, but that's just something we say to comfort ourselves. Objectively speaking, nothing matters. Regardless of the existence or nonexistence of God, there is a certain aspect of reality that remains to be explained because it is not something that is readily available to be understood. We are subjective creatures and we find meaning in the individual parts of life, but if we were suddenly to be as God is, an objective perspective which experiences all forms of existence, could we find meaning in any of it? When a man collects every single dollar in the entire world economy, what else is there to do except to give it away? Such is the matter of God, giving infinity to those with less.

There is something to be said of the duality we find in reality. If nothing changed, you would experience nothing, except it does change and so you do feel something. In a reality where nothing matters outside of your own receiving of life, the fact that it continues to change - apples fall, stars implode, atoms decay - is a marvelous wonder because it needn't do so. If the only thing that matters is the life we receive from God, the universe, or otherwise, then why don't we strive to expend all of our energies in experiencing it?

Euclid once said, "Handwriting is a spiritual designing, even though it appears by means of a material instrument."

Truly this is wisdom: to speak of an idea that feels true so deeply within its meaning that it might be readily agreed upon. When the aforementioned idea is inspected in greater detail, we find that it remains to be so.

What I seek to do is to describe that which is true from any point of vantage. It is a challenge to find such things to discuss, but it is an undertaking that both bolsters pride in the seeking individual and also humbles him due to the virtue of indescribability of which he hunts to acquire.

I dedicate myself to dedication itself; Happiness is happy, a rock is rock. Happiness can not be found in sadness except in contrast, and I foster an appreciation of this fact. Sadness is meant to be sad for the sake of it being so just as happiness does for itself, only in their own hues. Such things can be experienced in combination, but never as a truly homogeneous thing. If they were to become homogeneous, they would form something new and that new thing would be itself for the sake of it being so just as happiness or sadness. I do not mean to suggest that cause and effect do not take place, just that the cause should be appreciated as a cause and the effect as an effect.

That begs the question of what we are here for. What are we here for? That is the question of many lifetimes, perhaps all of them. Rather than seeking for an answer beyond, it may be beneficial to inquire within the question.

What? An implication that there is something which we may call "what." Are? An implication that there is a true state of being which applies to our "what." We? Us, me, you. Speaking of those who inquire into this problem. Here? Just as "what," it implies there is something, but also that the something is in a place which is not some other place. For? The thing we search for is implied by this final word. The matter that many people disagree on is whether we exist for something, or something exists for us. Are we below "for," like how in religion man is to God? Or are we above "for," searching to obtain something?

Each of these implications gives us a piece of the puzzle to put together. Finding answers within the questions is where we may use our intelligence to cultivate wisdom. Practicing this affair beyond our own minds allows for an individual to appear wiser than those who do not. A matter of "practice what you preach" but no one can hear you preach about what you are practicing. Similar to "how would you act if no one was watching?" No one can watch your mind except for you, and how you act within your own thoughts is the definition of who you are. The dissonance between your thoughts and actions is the integrity of your character.

The matters of good and evil are of little concern to those who have no interest in causing dilemmas of ethical scrutiny. Those who fear evil try to control it, those who detest it seek to destroy it, those who hate it want to fight it. A truly benevolent person sees evil and loves it just as they love goodness. Jesus is a perfect example. He (at least according to religious claims) did not hate anything, for he was the incarnation of the love of God in human form. Jesus did not hate those who did evil to him, instead he forgave them and loved them even at the very end of his life when he may have been absolutely justified to hate them. Good and evil are not requirements of moral philosophy, but rather implications of the branches of man who do not accept those things as they are.

Evil, if we may call it that, is a misguidance of those who had not the chance to learn to accept things as they are. Naturally, acceptance is the guide to peace, made especially apparent at the ends of our lives. If only we were to extend our love to all – including those who we apparently fear, detest, and hate - then maybe we could see that life does not have to be grim.

"We crave conflict," is what I've heard being said by people of many walks of life. But I think that's only partly true. There is a more basic part of conflict that, when removed from the negative term, debases conflict entirely. Change. We want change. Change can be a conflict, of course. Not all conflicts are change. I would say that change is a natural part of existence. But the moment when an individual craves a change from natural growth is the moment when conflict occurs. That craving to stop the growth is instinctual, as we all need a foundation to keep ourselves from slipping. Mistakes can be made so we all want a ground to catch us when we fall.

What if we make change a ground for standing upon? The grounds we currently gravitate towards are things that do not change. Stability is important, and the earth does a great job at providing stability. But as you walk towards the sand, stability seems to be a matter of faith. Any step may not be able to hold you, but you walk along anyway. The full commitment to release yourself from your desire of stability and become an exemplar of change is a level of faith which may allow you to then step onto the water. Though I do not recommend walking out into the ocean because it's just a metaphor.

3

I have a few goals in mind. One of which is a personal goal centered on my own understanding, the other is also a personal goal centered on the understanding of whoever is willing to consider my words. Such is my self-ordained task: to chase into the limits of infinity something that will never be known because that is the very nature of its being.

How is anyone to describe something which is indescribable? Diving deep into this idea we may find that there is more to say than one may realize. Exercising this question may broaden the horizons of your mind, or you may look at it and deem it useless, but regardless of what you think of it, try to take a moment to consider it important; Perhaps just lend me, for a moment, the benefits of your doubting.

Normally our understanding of reality is best described as binary. Mind and body. Heaven and earth. On and off. Something and nothing. Existence and nonexistence. But suppose for a moment that allowing ourselves to believe it is binary is what is limiting our perspective to something far greater.

Anselm fine-tuned an argument for the existence of God based on the idea that if God is the greatest conceivable being which no greater can be conceived, then God must exist not only in the mind but also in reality. The reason being that you can conceive of a greater being existing in both states if there is the idea of a being in one state. But there is a greater conceivable being than one that exists in both mind and reality.

Suppose that God is of self-sufficiency, able to exist without the need for anything else. Would that not suggest that God created Itself from nonexistence because God does not need anything to exist? And if this is true, God must also be of nonexistence. Though one may insert a comment about Schrödinger's cat, this case is not a superposition predicting either state. It is a more literal sense in which God does exist and also does not exist. If God knows all, God must also know how to not exist, how to become existent, how to reverse the process, and so on.

I do not mean to imply that a god of any particular religion, faith, or spiritual practice exists or doesn't, but instead I mean to suggest that our understanding of reality has been taught to us by ourselves, and we can learn to look for ideas beyond the ones we know of. All that needs to be done is to stand upon the mountain of thought and look out, look up. Understanding is a relativistic phenomenon.

4

There is a beautiful message in the song Luminol by Steven Wilson: "Here we all are, born into a struggle to come so far, but end up returning to dust." Such a beautiful way to put life into perspective. We are born into a world in which we scramble to survive. We try our hardest to be the best version of ourselves that we possibly can. Then we die, our bodies returning to the earth.

I often wonder whether I need to try my hand at anything, after all I will die one day. What is the point of trying so hard if one day I won't be able to try at all? But I think that's the beauty of it. There is no reason to be the best me, but I strive for it regardless.

I think it to be rather poetic for there to be meaning found in something where there seems to be none.

I could amass large amounts of wealth, pass it down to my children, and theirs, but it does not change the fact that we will all die. One way or another, none of the things that I own, nor the things I hold dear to me, will matter to me when I no longer live.

Dressing our dead in fancy suits and laying them ever so gingerly into padded boxes which took many hours to construct and decorate. This is what we do. It is for us that we do this, not for the dead, because of what use is any of those things to someone who has let go entirely the realm of worldliness?

Of course, I am not dead so who am I to say what the experience of death is like? No measurement or certainty of faith will ever tell me as a living person what being dead is like. Funnily enough, people still try to claim they know, even though they also live. To look for meaning in the end is only natural, and so it is reasonable to do so considering that it is unavoidable. But one day, perhaps consider not investing so much thought into the matters of death. Live. That's the gift that life gives you. Live as though it were the last life to have ever found meaning in anything. Feel your breath, your heartbeat, the blood pulsing through your veins.

Feel what it's like to experience living.

5

Every obstacle you face is a hurdle which hinders your growth, but overcoming it will make you stronger for the next. One such hurdle is that which pertains to the identity of the self. You may say, "I know who I am. I'm me!" But there is very little contemplation behind that kind of answer.

It is natural for people to think heavily on the lives they have lived when they become old. There is often little energy to do anything else. It is inevitable that people – aside from those who lose their mindful functions – will face themselves eventually. If it is only a matter of time before you are forced to look inward, why not start now? It would be wise to start early because a person is a very complex thing.

Where does one begin? The first question to be asked is a simple one: "Who am I?" This question may be satisfied at some point in your life, or maybe there will never be an answer. What comes of the question is for you to decide.

So who am I? Materialists may give you the idea that you are your body. Though it is true that you control it, you are not the only organism to adhere to the fact of being your body. The body is made of an incredibly large number of cells. In fact, there are more cells in the average human body than there are galaxies in the known universe.

If you cut off all of your limbs, granting your body time to compensate for survival, you will find yourself still living. Certainly the identity of which you are synonymous must be a part of you which cannot be removed from yourself. The part of you that even if you were to remain living after removing all of your body, you would still not be able to remove yourself from yourself.

Where can I find myself? The best bet for a physical location is the brain. The control center is where it would make the most sense to find the pilot. But is that really me? I have the ability to identify myself as something beyond my own body, and it doesn't entirely make sense for nature to allow such a thing.

Is my ability to recognize myself as something beyond my human biology a byproduct of developed emotions such as sympathy, empathy, and compassion? It certainly is advantageous to feel these things, it improves chances of survival after all.

Does the nature of reflection reveal anything about the self? Or is reflection merely a byproduct of having physical form? I cannot say that I know for certain. One thing is certain though; I exist. If I did not exist, I would have nothing to say or do, you would not be reading this, I would not have written this, and my landlord would not be receiving rent from a young man living in this small apartment. The fact that I perceive anything at all is a fact of my existence. My experience of it however, is subjective.

Can I truly know who I am if my experience is subjective?

This is a much harder question to find an answer to. Imagine for a moment that you are a grain of sand. For all we know, a grain of sand could contain a vast universe at a scale that is incomprehensibly small. Say that it does exactly that. It would make sense for you to identify yourself as the entirety of the universe on that grain of sand because you are the grain of sand and the universe that makes it up.

But this analogy fails to respond to cries like, "even a grain of sand is made of smaller parts, so how small can it be before it is no longer a grain of sand?" Strangely this is almost the exact same question as, "who am I?"

We know that there is an "I" because of the fact that we know anything at all. This concludes the latter part of the question, "am I?" The majority of the strain is emphasized by "who" it is that we search for. Now I must discuss the problem with looking for yourself, which is only a problem in the sense that it is a sort of puzzle to put together.

Many people associate themselves with their personality, and it certainly makes sense to do so. These are the sorts of people who usually either believe that the self is determined by actions or it is revealed by their aesthetic style. This is in stark contrast to those who remain steadfast thinking that they are an object to be recognized.

But when the factors which foster such qualities of individual flavor are removed, we are left devoid of personality. What then? Where is the self if it is not personality? I am more confident in proclaiming that I am something that can be found because I know my personality is not what I am. My personality is not the being which looks in on itself, it is more like a bag of tea leaves which gives the water its flavorful properties. If that is the case then am I the water, God the pourer?

Still, it remains open to be answered. "Who?" At this point, the only thing I can do is to be a bit pretentious and make proclaimed claims. Every invention of human history required at least a little bit of pretentiousness, otherwise nothing would be invented. You must assume that there is something to be made or found despite the information you currently have. The lightbulb was improved upon many times because someone believed there was a better way. So let us plunge into our pretentious minds for a moment and assume that we will certainly find the answer to the question.

I must not be my body, at least not fully because I can identify myself as something beyond the fact of biology. I must be able to interact with the physical in some way, and all interactions of any kind are physical in the sense that there are reactions between two continuities. Take photosynthesis for example. Photons react with plants to provide them with energy, but photons aren't matter. They make a physical interaction despite not being matter. This pattern can be applied to the idea of the soul. If there is a soul, it is likely some sort of energy, like light, which interacts with the physical.

Our perception of the universe, as mentioned earlier, is subjective and incomplete. Even the instruments which we use to perceive things beyond our own senses can show us a limited amount. This is for two reasons: 1) it may be impossible to perceive all layers of existence because they are too far beyond the reach of the ability to perceive and 2) our tools to perceive the universe are limited by our imaginations and the matter with which such tools can be created.

Even if we were able to think of a tool to sense an unsensible thing, it would have to be created using the matter that exists. It is impossible to utilize matter that does not exist because of the very fact of its lack of existence. The point is that it may be impossible for us to learn of the nature of the soul because it is beyond the realm of measurement.

If there is a soul, is that the "who" in our question? Can it be accurately stated that the true self is the soul? At first glance this makes sense. In fact, it makes sense even after deep contemplation. But there is an intrusive thought that follows if you remain in the solitude of your mind for long enough. "What if I am not my soul nor my body?" This is a question that may seem absurd at first, but upon closer inspection you might find that there is more to this question than just the implication that you are something else.

This question is one of those rare, yet simple, veils to a deeper truth. This is a question which opens the door to the eldritch plane of knowledge. What I mean to say is that it is a question more intimate than "who am I?" but cannot be pursued in any logical means. But remember my note on pretentiousness. You can always approach the question even if you never find the answer.

Perhaps we can try to listen carefully to those who believe in the idea of actions revealing the self. The soul and body interact to create consciousness, your consciousness. If we use the aforementioned ideology, we can identify ourselves with action. Interactions are a byproduct of actions, but are themselves actions. It may be reasonable then to identify the self as the interaction that happens between body and soul. This implies that you are a pattern rather than an object.

Let us think for a moment about what being a pattern is like. An example which I will use is one I heard from an old recording of a lecture given by a rather impressively intelligent man named Alan Watts. I do not remember if he produced the example or if he also heard it somewhere, but I will explain it anyway.

Imagine you have a very long rope, made that way by tying the ends of smaller cloths together. This is similar imagery to a handkerchief rope that a clown or magician coughs up as a part of their act. Each cloth is made of a different fabric in this case – silk, cotton, polyester, satin, hemp, and so on. These represent the matter of the universe. Now twist a loop into the rope so that you can move the loop along the rope by running your finger along it. That loop is you. Not the rope that makes up the loop, but the loop pattern.

One could say that the person holding the loop along the rope is representative of the soul, the knots being obstacles, the fabrics as changes in perception, and of course the rope as the physical matter. That pattern which is the interaction between your finger and the rope - the loop - is the happening that can be identified as the self.

"Who am I?" I am a pattern in the universe. We could stop there, most people who get to this point do. Certainly this answer would satisfy the majority of people who want to look for themselves. Although I could stop there, I have a particular personal philosophy which prevents me from stopping at any conclusion. If the universe truly is as incomprehensible as it can be imagined to be, there must be something even deeper than this. I would not blame you if you decided to stop reading because from here on out the concepts I will suggest are the kinds of things you do not want to think about alone in the darkest hours of the morning.

Scientifically it is possible that there are an uncountable number of universes. Imagine yourself at the beach, crouched down to observe the sand. Now imagine each and every single grain to be a universe. Don't stop at the beach, think of the vast deserts of the world, such as the Sahara. All of those exist within the larger universe which we call our own. Now look out to the stars and imagine that this universe is also a grain of sand on a beach or in a desert. It is possible that there are just as many universes which you have contemplated this concept as there are universes in which a single grain of sand is in a slightly different spot. Now imagine that there are just as many universes that create patterns identical to you. Imagine that not all universes create people based on an interaction between soul and body. There are an infinite number of possibilities not only in the nature of each universe, but also groups of universes and even groups of those groups and so on.

An existential crisis can be very intimidating, but by using your ability to apply meaning to life you can "be not afraid" so to speak. What does your life mean in such an unfathomable infinity?

The power of subjective perspective is that it is a perspective that belongs only to you and objective reality. Objective reality can be interpreted as the universe, multiverse, nature, or God (although not limited to just the Christian god). Whatever it is that you choose to believe objectivity to be, it is of less concern to figure out what it is than it is to interact with it, just like putting a loop in the rope.

It is impossible to know things that are impossible to know because of that very fact. Just like the tools we create to measure things we cannot perceive, we ourselves are limited by our imagination and the bodies we control. The universe holds an infinite amount of information and we have a skull which keeps our brains from infinitely expanding. We will never know the extent of infinity because there will always be more to know.

What does one do when there is far too much to do or know? Be you. Live, because there will only ever be one instance in which you exist in exactly the time, place, and way that you do now. There might be infinite numbers of you in the cosmos, but only you will ever be the you that you are. Maybe you will be reincarnated to relive the life you lived, but even if that is true you only exist this time *this time*.

6

There arises an issue after some time being alone. There is a strong desire to be around other people, even if you do not recognize this fact. A great loneliness seeps from the center of the chest distracting the body of other needs, like eating or exercise. After an extended period of loneliness, there comes a depression which can either be incredibly self-destructive, or if the individual understands what is going on it may be used as a motivator.

The feeling of being alone evolves steadily over time as you become familiar with it. At first it may feel like a bird being freed from its cage, soaring into distant skies. This feeling is usually what makes venturing off alone feel so desirable. But even birds begin to tire and they must eat and drink and rest to continue their way of life.

That feeling of being completely unbound gradually wanes over time and the mind begins to settle. But in this case, the bird has flown very far and cannot find faces which it recognizes. It must find nourishment so it can return to the skies but the nourishment it needs is from the faces it cannot find. So now there is a new feeling that bubbles within. It grows until finally the bird decides to use its legs for once, to look at the ground from a much closer perspective.

By doing this, the bird finds new faces amongst the underbrush. Faces that may have never been seen if it were not for its decision to choose a new path. But the faces it meets here, though it may be fond of them in some way or another, are not faces that belong to the path that the bird seeks. A bird must fly.

The individual seeks in others something that can only be found within themselves. It is the realization that the object of their desire comes from within that allows them to begin climbing a new tree to take flight from. But this transition is where many split up. Some climb the tree and look out into the sky remembering the terrible loneliness they felt when they fell from it. Some look out at the sky and appreciate it for what it was, inevitably returning to the ground. Others still, look up and down and realize that their venture into the free winds will always return them to the ground, and so they soar as high as they possibly can.

I may be incredibly vague in describing this with a metaphorical tone, and that is no mistake. It is up to you to determine meaning for yourself. However I feel I should also discuss this in a more formal tone.

I have spent a very lengthy time alone. In the beginning it felt like freedom. I slowed down to cherish my freedom and I utilized my time with that appreciation. Over time the mind can be discouraged by the circumstances at hand, and the search for a renewed sense of freedom begins. Except it isn't quite the same freedom that I was searching for. I was looking for a new chapter to signify the next part of my life.

Once again, my mind became weary and I began to feel awful. I wanted to share my achievements with those closest to me, but I had decided to venture off for a new path. After a while, I realized that the dedication required to continue on this new path I had chosen was one that needed support from others, not just my own will. Though my will was strong I have found that even the strongest of wills can be whittled down to nearly nothing if it is not cared for.

The care that a person requires is not just physical - like food, water, exercise, learning, growth, and gratification - but emotional as well (I am aware that emotions are chemical processes, but they have a certain complexity to them which sets them apart from more mechanical needs). Friends, family, community. These are aspects of life that care for the emotional needs of an individual. Without them, the individual becomes less and less stable.

With enough time, I accepted my circumstances of loneliness, but acceptance does not remove the issue. Acceptance in this context is only the recognition of the fact that you know the circumstances are as they are. I decided to give myself a new change. I decided that I would no longer be lonely, and though the only path out of loneliness would be long and arduous, it would be far more beneficial to choose this path over the path I had previously chosen. I have already reaped benefits from this new path and here I am, still alone in my apartment. I might take it to be a sign. All that's needed is a change in perspective.

7

How can I pull meaning into my life? For someone who has little to no purpose outside of himself, it is incredibly difficult to find a reason to do anything at all. The gratification of self-improvement does not compare to the praise that a second individual might give if they found the first being productive. So how can I feel good about doing this alone?

There is plenty of practical advice for this out there. Do one small thing a day that is outside your comfort zone. Try one difficult thing every other day. That sort of thing. But attempting to commit to that sort of thing when you have no one cheering you on is incredibly difficult. Sure, those things do certainly have an impact, but how can you keep interest in that commitment?

Here is my solution. I begin with a small list of things I want to do. This list is composed of simple actions that provide a sense of meaning to otherwise mundane tasks. For example, in most religious practices there is an act of prayer before meals and going to bed. Even if you are not religious, expressing some form of thanks or appreciation for the food or even the circumstances that allow you the comfort to sleep can make these tasks feel more important.

This list can extend to other things besides unavoidable needs, though it is best to start using such rituals in tandem with something that is unavoidable for the sake of habit. Some things I include are: count up by ten from any number upon waking, take the time to look at nature every single day, check my mind and my heart before leaving home, and make as many conscious decisions as I can every day.

By applying these little rituals I find myself feeling less hopeless. It feels as though there is care involved; my life feels like it is being tended to. This incredibly simple practice of creating little ritual actions for your day is so simple that it may be easy to overlook. I didn't even think about it for the long time I've been alone until just before I wrote this.

And I should clarify that I do not commit myself completely to the items on my list, just that I put effort into doing things that I am not required to do.

We are creatures who search for meaning and I feel as though sometimes we can forget that the meaning we search for is something that we ourselves create.

8

Sometimes I wander outside my apartment to the unfamiliar place which it happens to be found in. I take many steps into the woods along the man made trail provided to me.

I stop to listen. I listen to the wind and the birds, the rustling of leaves. Bugs buzz around me, a train rolls along the tracks in the distance. A calmness sweeps over me as I begin to realize that I am listening to the world happen without my intervention. I do not hold the responsibility to make any significant mark on the page of humanity's book of life, but to make a mark on any page at all is an achievement which is telling of human nature.

I wander into the woods, guided by the trail, and I connect with nature. A very interesting thing that I discovered while on my own is that connecting to things saturates you in your own way of being you. As we grow older, we might look back on our past and connect to things that we think of fondly. I used to draw a lot as a young kid, and I stopped for quite a while. But now I picked the pencil back up and enjoy it just as much or even more than I used to. I've connected to my inner child by enjoying the things that I did in childhood.

Choosing to connect with anything, or anyone, is a choice that, when done without fear of regret, can deliver great joy and immense amounts of meaningful time. Even if I work a lot, I still manage to find joy in my time. Every moment I spend away from the activities I want to do draws me stronger towards them. I am happy for the moments away from what I enjoy just as I am for the moments that I enjoy.

Sure, there are definitely things that seem unfair in the world and I commend those who work hard to make life seem fair. Personally, I take life as my given circumstances; the only resources I use are the ones that I am able to obtain. Surely I could work towards change in the world, but as an individual my ideas are not very effective in terms of societal restructuring. I am far more versed in the search for meaning in a life with seemingly none.

When an artist finds a way of expressing themselves, they may hone their skill in producing pieces which resemble that expression. This is called developing a style. I use this idea in the way I live life by searching for the things I might be decent at and then I develop skills in regards to those things. What am I good at? Questioning everything and looking at things from new perspectives. So what skills do I practice? I am always trying to develop a loquacious vocabulary to better describe my thoughts, but I also practice drawing to view as many perspectives as possible.

You may not be good at the thing you are trying to be good at, but if you enjoy doing it don't be discouraged. If it brings you happiness then what reason is there to stop? If you try something new occasionally, even if you are unable to do most things, you may find something that you enjoy and maybe you'll even be good at. Try new things.

Most of all, connect. By connecting to something, you will find new things to do and learn about. You'll develop skills you may not have ever developed if you didn't try it. Just remember to enjoy the time away from your interests because it makes them all the more enticing.

9

Sitting alone in a quiet studio apartment gets to be harmful to the psyche after some time. I've used my time in various ways and I am always looking for new ways to use it. I've listened to a great deal of music, played a variety of games, leafed through many pages, scrolled through too many videos, and whittled down my pencils after excessive use.

Trying to keep yourself busy is not always the best idea. Doing too much can overstimulate you. Burnout is especially dangerous if you do not have anyone to tell you to get up and do something because there's the chance you might not even get up that day. Or the next. I don't recommend trying to overload yourself, but having nothing to do isn't so bad either.

Sometimes I like to sit and wait. Not for anything in particular to happen, but just until the waiting is no longer top priority. I observe my living space, I look out the window, I sit and watch the world around me until the world decides it wants to do something with me again. That's the feeling I get when I sit in my chair on a quiet day with nothing to do. Not everyone in the world has the luxury of spending their time like this which is why I stop to appreciate it as much as I can.

With enough time spent in this way, it can feel as though your interest in doing other things increases. Think of it like this, the dust built up in a room is constantly kicked around by you going about your business. You won't ever notice how dusty the room actually is until you stop and sit for a while to let the dust settle. So let the dust settle for a moment and see what happens.

10

It is common for philosophers to consider matters of aesthetics to be unimportant when looking for answers to their questions. There is something that I found to be quite interesting despite this.

Assume that there is an objective force - God, gods, the universe or even its properties - which is present in all things. There is one thing that is consistent in all things despite the vast number of properties different things have. They all have some sort of simulative existence in the universe. The same is true of ideas. All ideas that have ever existed are based upon the information within the universe itself, because the body is in it.

When looking at the branches of philosophy - epistemology, metaphysics, ethics, logic, and aesthetics - we can analyze the information each branch considers and determine their function.

Epistemology is meant to discover the ways we understand information in the first place. We can ask, why is it that we must understand things in the first place? Metaphysics brings the birth and functionality of the universe itself into question. People often argue for or against the existence of a god or gods but it distracts from the focus of metaphysics which is to better understand the workings of existence. Why do we want to know how the universe works or how it started? Ethics is the attempt to force a structure onto the chaos of the universe by placing value on the social circumstance. Though it is productive of us to maintain relatively good ethical values, why can't we live understanding morality inherently from within ourselves? Logic allows us to better analyze the world around us using the measurements of our observation. Logic is a purely functional branch of philosophy and is more of a tool to be used than a set of ideas to be learned.

What about aesthetics? For me I find that this is the most important branch of all, contrasted to many philosophers who think otherwise. Aesthetics is generally a way to understand art, to find the value or non-value in art which we create for each other. But there is one thing that sets it apart from the other branches.

By using branches of philosophy as pieces of the whole puzzle rather than separate practices, we can find our ideas to be generated in a far more complex and interesting way. My way of doing philosophy applies aesthetics to all the other branches of philosophy. After all, the primary note on aesthetics is perspective, subjectivity, and objectivity which is why it is set apart from the others. Aesthetics is the tool we use to generate new ideas by applying new perspectives.

When applying aesthetics to the whole of philosophy, one can begin to think of the universe as the ultimate art piece which no other can compare. There is one thing to note when suggesting any idea which is the fact that your experience and understanding of any idea is subjective. Objectivity is for the perspective that contains all other perspectives.

Sure, we find many of our experiences to overlap enough for us to understand the world from a larger scale - we all share words that we collectively agree have certain meanings, for example - but we often fail to understand the world inwardly.

By observing yourself as inwardly as possible, keeping in mind that even your inner self is just as much a part of the universe as the world outside of your mind, you may find that there is something more to be found than just your memories and calculations. After a deep and long contemplative adventure of your mind, you will begin to remove patterns from systems of existence and apply them to other things. Of course you may make a mistake on what patterns are there to be recognized, but error can reveal a new path for you to travel along.

I realize I am very vague in my descriptions of this process, and that is purposeful. You should take all of my words in a way that makes sense to you. My words are not actually my words, just impressions of much more complex ideas which I cannot confine myself to words to describe. Regardless, I think it may be useful to give an example.

Study the patterns that are shared between the larger cosmos and the realm of the atomic scale. Look at the processes of converting nutrients into energy and byproducts such as our breathing and photosynthesis. The shapes of the trees look awfully similar to the nervous system and also the pathways within the lungs which take in air and even the cardiovascular system.

By looking at the shapes and functions of things you will find that there are some shapes in the world which will always have certain functions as well as certain functions that require certain shapes. This is looking through the lens of aesthetic philosophy to look at reality.

Why is it that we must understand things in the first place? Our brains are of the capacity to search for patterns which allow us to understand and it is the most complex organic object in the universe. It computes the universe because it is of the shape to do so. It is the exact same property as a cup being shaped to hold liquids in the presence of gravity. It is shaped the way it is in order to fulfill a function. What function? Calculation and understanding which are unique properties that are found only in similar structural shapes to the brain.

Why do we want to know the nature of the universe or how it started? Initially, curiosity is the driver of such a question but as one is forced to address themselves in the quiet of their mind, it becomes a path towards finding a purpose in life. Of course everyone disagrees on the nature of the universe; everyone finds a different purpose to life just like a group of individuals interpreting a painting from their own perspectives. The beginning of the universe is not subjective, but because it happened so long ago we are greatly prone to error. It's just like connecting two distant dots with a straight line; if you are off by even one degree, you will completely miss the other dot. The only way to know how it started is to have zero percent error, otherwise the dot will be missed.

To come back to an earlier question, why can't we have an inherent sense of morality? I have found that ethical understanding increases when using aesthetic practice. Moral issues are often debated to be black or white, even gray issues are determined to be made of smaller black and white characteristics. The debate of whether or not a complicated issue is right or wrong seems to fade when considering all of existence as a piece of art. Art is preserved to inspire more art, though eventually it will fade away. The value that is placed on it is entirely made up, but it is because we are the ones placing value on it that makes it special to us. Unfortunately I need to use a moral issue to make an example of. Abortion has cases in which it makes sense and cases in which it does not. The correctness of whether it is or is not done is not objective because human abortions are only in the thoughts of human minds. People fight for what they believe is right, but objectively the only "right" thing to do is to be existent in the canvas of the cosmos. Abortion can be thought through logically in the context of societal norms, and it may even be the case that thousands of years from now, it would be improper to keep a child at all. Ethics is just as subjective as any piece of art, and to deny such a thing is to deny reality.

As a final note, just as I mentioned before, logic is a tool rather than a branch of knowledge. The combination of aesthetics and logic is what allows for a much more comprehensive understanding of a broad range of things. By using logic to measure and gain reference for how the universe may objectively be, we can give structure to our subjective understanding of the world around us.

The thing which I find even more fascinating is the fact that there are sections of your brain, the left and right, which correspond to logical structure and aesthetic perspective. In my mind, all other branches of philosophy are more like labels on ideas which have particular tendencies to do certain things. This is why I view aesthetics to be the most important branch of philosophy. This is why I often clash with the ideas that presume to have any one thing figured out.

It is true that humanity has a great deal of information at their disposal, understanding the patterns of the world in a way to progress towards technological efficiency. The fact of the matter is that all we are doing is recognizing these patterns, describing them with patterns of language, and recognizing similar patterns. Apart from our familiarity of the patterns we know of, we know nothing at all. There is not a single example in which I cannot reduce to mere patterns.

But isn't that the beauty of it all? We are like a surfer riding a wave, we ride the patterns until we arrive at the shore. Though it comes to an end, there will be many other waves to come.

11

There is not enough time or energy to be able to contemplate all things. But we can at least make it easier for each other. Sitting alone for the time I've lived as an independent adult has given me a great deal of wisdom in the areas of which I lack proper resources.

Alone, I can only think about thoughts of my own. With the internet, I am able to greatly expand the number of things which I can contemplate. But without proper conversation, I cannot come to accurate conclusions because the reasoning I hold is self-contained. I certainly have had conversations which were rather productive, but sitting once again in my quiet solitude I find that such productivity only lasts outside of these walls.

Over time, philosophers have viewed and considered the works of other philosophers, morphed those ideas into their own, cited them, published them. Those published ideas are then put to the same cyclical process, almost as if the ideas were in their own state of samsara, waiting to find their true identities before they can ever be let go of. Generating new ideas is incredibly difficult because even ideas produced alone may match perfectly to the ideas of another individual from another place or time, your experiences never even recognizing each other.

I had this experience during an intro class to philosophy in the fall of 2023. My idea was that it would be possible for God to be the ultimate singular being only if God was literally the entirety of existence on all levels. This was a conclusion I came to through the study of the nature of what God is meant to be, but it was, as I found out nearing the end of that class, not an original idea. In fact, we can put a label on this idea; pantheism.

So it is clear that it is unlikely that anyone will come up with an original conceptual idea, but that should not be justification to stop trying. If anything is for certain, it's that no one knows everything. As a collective mass of minds we can do what it is that we were designed or evolved to do. We must communicate with each other in order to grow.

Even a single conversation is enough to greatly increase your own understanding of the world around you. One brain can do great things, but a second brain can halve the work required to come to more accurate conclusions.

In connection to this theme, it may be beneficial to learn about lottocracies. I know I said I would not speak on political matters, but I discuss this subject as a means to present new ideas for the future. We should not think that our current reality is going to be a permanent one.

So what is a lottocracy? It is a form of government which is governed by randomly appointed people. In such a government, a number of people could be chosen to make a decision with the guidance of experts on the subject. Any person could be chosen at random for this decision making, and so it would be of great importance in such a government to make decisions based on the best desired outcome rather than an outcome that benefits the individuals making such decisions. The individuals would not be doing this task as a career and so forming policies which benefit themselves in such a position would be impossible, especially because the group discussing the decision must come to an agreement. Even better, the group chosen would be of variety rather than of a certain sort.

Would such a government ever come to fruition in the modern day? It is doubtful. Although, it certainly is a possibility. For those frustrated with current forms of government, perhaps this is a light in the darkness. I am not saying that lottocracy is the only possible option, but it certainly seems like a very good one.

I strongly advocate for the progression of an efficiently growing human race, but there are many issues - mostly caused by humans themselves - which hinder such efficiencies. Material processing emissions, for example, pollute the air and water. This isn't exactly good for the well-being of those who created the processes nor those who live in spite of them.

Now I must remind you that I am not calling for some sort of mutiny, but I do suggest that we look for more meaningful ways to communicate and govern ourselves. Certainly if the human race is in charge of itself it can think of a way to provide for its entire body of individuals.

The world is full of seemingly useless information. For example, the word vegetable is actually a culinary term usually used to refer to plant foods with characteristics in contrast to fruits. Vegetable is not a botanical term and so vegetables do not technically exist. You could go throughout your entire life not knowing this information without any issue, so it's basically a useless fact outside of the field of botany.

But instead of looking at the information itself, what would happen if we looked at the characteristics of it? What does the information tell us implicitly?

Language is a good place to start. It seems as though people make words for a specific function, but when it is learned by others who do not understand why it was used in the first place, the word is used in new ways. This seems to happen a lot in English, but naturally I would assume other languages run into this sometimes, too. All that is needed is for someone to use a word in a new context, a task that is so often practiced that we often refer to it as poetry.

There are likely many words in the English language with a similar circumstance to vegetable. Each word refers to something specific yet we are able to draw associations to similar concepts to reuse the word in a different context.

The function of language is not to get super technical, though you certainly can play that game. Language is a tool for communication and as long as the people you are conversing with understand enough of what you are trying to convey, it is being used successfully.

But language is an external tool that you process internally. When I say up we both imagine what we associate that word with. What I imagine is different from what you imagine, and that's for every single word. Every single word in this entire text has a meaning, but I am not explaining what runs through my mind for each and every word. I am merely using many strings of words in hopes that those who have internal associations to the words I use will understand something about what I am attempting to convey.

Now, when you live primarily in silence you begin to play little games in your mind. One of these is what I think is referred to as a mind palace, though I am not entirely sure I am using this exact technique. What I like to do is think about something, like a pencil for example, and I try to think about how many things I can relate it to. Writing, language, drawing, pictures, books, graphite, lead, minerals, wood, plastic, eraser, create, destroy, tool, use, and the list continues. Over time, I begin to reuse associated words for other objects, which brings the two objects closer in my mind.

Thinking activities are very interesting because in order to think, neurons are fired. If neurons are fired frequently, the brain will begin to make pathways to reduce the energy required to fire those neurons. So if I were to take two ideas that would never even be considered in the same day and I repeatedly think about those two things back and forth, I would create a physical connection in my brain associating those completely unrelated ideas. So if I were to tell someone I relate those two things, they would think I'm losing my grip but in reality all I did was use a memory technique that they likely haven't done. At least for those two ideas.

I think it's quite funny that it is easier to remember ideas when you associate them with unrelated things. I have tried to remember birthdays by relating the date to the person it belongs to, but I found it much easier to remember if I gave the date some other absurd association. For example, I know some people have a birthday on the 23rd, and a movie I remember fairly vividly is The Number 23 with Jim Carrey. He obsesses over the number in the movie, and it helps me to remember things very easily when they relate to the number 23.

You control your own mind, take a moment to think about what it is capable of.

13

You are responsible for your own development. Of course, only after you gain the ability to take care of yourself. When you are able to do that, you are accountable for your own development. It is up to you to decide to take people's words seriously or dismiss them, so others cannot take the credit for what you become. However, this also means that you are not responsible for the growth of others, aside from maybe your son's or daughter's development into their self-sufficient stage of life.

Anyone can tell you to eat healthier, do better at your job, look for meaning in your life, but the choice to do so ultimately falls upon your own shoulders. Your choices are your own, and they will always be yours for whatever reason or lack thereof you justify them with.

Even though you are the sole decider of your actions does not mean you can't listen to others. We all share the same experience of being alive inside our own individual bodies, but the fact that we are all in a body tells us that we all have at least a little bit of a frame of reference for the experiences of other people. What someone says may be incredibly insightful to you even if it doesn't seem that way to them. The same is true in the opposite direction, though that is no excuse to assume that you have a better understanding of something than others.

I believe I understand a number of things pretty well, but I also keep in mind that we do not actually know for sure how the universe works. I understand everything that I know from my perspective alone. I can imagine other perspectives, but that is a phenomenon that happens inside my own mind, so how am I to be sure I am not just seeing my own perspective from a different angle?

14

Silence. The still air echoes sounds that are normally indistinguishable from silence. Louder still are the endless words and sounds that no one besides I can hear. I express those things in the form of words on the page, unveiling my innermost compassion for the world around me.

I have learned many things from living alone, far from the people I care about the most.

It is far easier for us to see things in contrast than in comparison. Though the grass is a beautiful green on the other side of the fence, the grass is just as green on this side of it, too. The great blue sky may be clear and beautiful throughout the year in some parts of the world, and yet it is always going to be raining somewhere else. You may forget how beautiful either of those things are until you experience the opposite.

People are people, no matter how you might view them. They say a bunch of words to describe themselves and who they are, but an understanding of the self is not something that can be accurately portrayed to its fullest extent. You will only ever be able to perceive others from your own point of view because everything you know comes from your perception of them. Still, we are all connected in that we share this experience. The only difference between us is the angle that we have on life.

Sometimes people do things that seem meaningless. There is no inherent value in doing some things, but people still do them. Perhaps that little thing means a lot to them for one reason or another. It is not the place of any other person to set a standard for what you should find value in. What you value relies on your perspective on life.

Many people have the same passions as other people, but that is no reason to feel dissuaded from your own. The universe repeats many patterns; it is not the job of those patterns to be unique, it is their job to be beautiful from where they are. Even if you find an identical copy of yourself, they will never be beautiful as you are, only beautiful as they are.

15

Not all things need to be understood. Actually, nothing needs to be understood. It is out of the desire to continue forward that we try to understand things, but it is not a requirement; we could just stop learning and go extinct if we wanted to. We could do may different things if we wanted to do them, but here we are doing what we're doing right now.

Nothing is required to be done yet we still choose to do. Many people are in power in this world, and they usually take their positions incredibly seriously. Quite ironic considering the fact that it is not specifically tasked of anyone to take charge. Sure, we need systems that work well enough in place if we want to continue to survive, but that doesn't mean we are limited to the systems that have or still do exist. Even then, we could live life like a free-for-all, but we don't because it's irrational.

Why is it irrational to drop all formal responsibilities and play the game of survival of the fittest? We wouldn't be able to survive very long if we decided to do things that way, and it would put all things at a net greater difficulty. So it seems as though rationality has a stronger bond to collective survival over individual survival.

We choose to survive, the universe does not demand it. It is out of our collective rationality that we go on living as a species.

Nothing you will ever do is required of you to be done. But the same goes for every single individual who has and will ever live. But that's the beauty of being creatures with free will, we can do whatever it is that we want to do because there is nothing that is required of us. We build and destroy simply for the sake of doing something. Well, that and to stabilize a future for ourselves, but that is also arguably just something that we decided to do.

What happens when you apply this idea practically in your life? It illuminates a path guided by the understanding that everything you do is chosen to be done by you.

The burden of your actions lies solely on your own shoulders. You become aware of the fact that you are in control of your future. Sure, people have their lives forced into directions they did not plan for, but people are not identifiable as their circumstances.

I am certain that.

~~~

Sometimes you need to break the rules of life in order to live. There may be a rule in place to protect you or to be of some other purpose, but sometimes a broken rule is not the worst option. I refer to the sorts of rules that serve no other purpose than to raise the chances of happiness or safety but are not guaranteed. Or the rules which are not required but improve efficiency of the setting.

There may be some cases in which breaking such rules are desirable.

The entirety of my writing which was produced during my time in my small apartment is not a collection of words to be taken in too serious of a light. My circumstances may have altered my perception of all things I described, thus I write a reflection in lieu of my attempt at portrayals of ideas I wouldn't stop to be more complete than they actually were.

Ideas are just like people; they live and grow into something seemingly different constantly. Just as the light bulb filament began as a carbonized cotton thread, useful for perhaps a night or two; a man must begin as a thoughtless boy curious for the things he does not know.

Every moment is a moment passed. We lose time all the time only to receive more of it, until we have none left. We learn to know, know to act, act to teach, teach to love, love to live, live to die.

Life is like art, or the making of it. Sometimes it's ugly, but we can learn from the ugliness to steer us towards finer things. Mistakes are opportunities to create things in a positive light, if only a recognition of that mistake is made. No single art piece is perfect except when considering that each one was made with the intent to convey itself as it is or in contrast to something else.

Every life is unique, even in conformity. Though it may feel as though every day is the same, either to days you've experienced or to ones being experienced elsewhere, it is time experienced through the eyes in your own skill which makes it yours.

The darkest days are those which you chose not to follow the light.

I had given up on publishing my book because I thought of my words as incomplete in some way. I was dissatisfied with the state of it all. How might a man as young as myself convey wisdom he isn't sure he has? But it doesn't matter that I'm not old and gray, or that I haven't followed through with the modern path of schooling to learn the complete works of the most respected philosophers.

Philosophy as a practice should not be taken in such a serious tone all the time. Stoicism is not always practical in every matter. We don't always have to ask whether our actions are right or wrong because sometimes our emotions are stronger than our need of morality.

One of the hundreds or even thousands of habitats we have destroyed as a species just to erect a factory or farms in their place? Have we ever considered it wrong to prioritize any one thing over another? Naturally there are those who do question these things but it is all for naught as those with the power to make change or those in charge of the fate of our world.

Frustration seeps down within the minds of those without power, birthing the anarchist point of view. Change! They cry, we know it can be better! Is it ever better? At what point can we say that we have achieved this "better" we long for so dearly?

The stars. They move so incredibly fast and we cannot know where they actually are until their light travels unimaginable distances to us. Balls of burning gas larger than our entire planet, even our entire solar system, let along the Sun. Massive distillery explosions and void like vortexes we call black holes, for lack of fancier words. We know nothing of what happens in our own universe until it has already happened.

Abby buzzes, dancing in the light breeze. A chip sings through the leaves of the trees. You touch the just barely dried earth between the blades of grass. Pick a blade. Put it between your fingers. Blow. It whistles.

Despite everything, you are here. You could be dead, you could have never been born. But you're reading this so I know you're here. You are. That's all that matters. What you decide to do with that is your choice, there are no universal rules that can change what you decide to do. People still run at public pools despite the signs warning against it.

Your life is your canvas, your abilities the paint, you the artist. So pick that blade of grass and blow at it between your fingers. Laugh because it sounds funny, smile because you can, watch the clouds change colors with the sky as the sun sets, draw lines between the stars, and dream of all the beautiful things on your canvas.

www.ingramcontent.com/pod-product-compliance
Lightning Source LLC
Chambersburg PA
CBHW020041040426
42331CB00030B/452